BRITISH ARMY UNIFORMS IN COLOR

BRITISH ARMY UNIFORMS IN COLOR

AS ILLUSTRATED BY JOHN McNEILL,
ERNEST IBBETSON, EDGAR A. HOLLOWAY
AND HARRY PAYNE
c. 1908-1919

PETER HARRINGTON

Schiffer Military History
Atglen, PA

The paintings reproduced here for the first time are from the Anne S.K. Brown Military Collection at the Brown University Library in Providence, Rhode Island, USA. This collection is one of the largest of its kind devoted to the history and more particularly the iconography of soldiers and soldiering of all nations from circa 1500 to the twentieth century. It consists of over 16,000 prints, drawings, paintings and watercolors, over 13,000 printed books, and thousands of albums, sketchbooks, scrapbooks, and portfolios, not to mention 6,000 toy soldiers. Donated by Mrs. John Nicholas Brown of Providence in 1981, it is now housed in the John Hay Library of Brown University, and is used by scholars, publishers, documentary and film makers. It continues to grow through new acquisitions and gifts.

The collection includes numerous military postcards including the famous uniform cards published by the well-known British military publishing company of Gale & Polden. The original paintings which were reproduced on these postcards are hard to find today but a number of these are reproduced here and show the skill and effort which went into making every image. The artists represented were some of the leading military illustrators of their day, and their talents can be readily appreciated. They have documented in fine detail the impressive dress uniforms worn by the British Army in the years leading up to the Great War in 1914.

Book design by Robert Biondi.

Copyright © 2001 by Peter Harrington.
Library of Congress Catalog Number: 00-108163.

Printed in China.
ISBN: 0-7643-1302-9

We are always looking for people to write books on new and related subjects. If you have an idea for a book, please contact us at the address below.

Published by Schiffer Publishing Ltd.
4880 Lower Valley Road
Atglen, PA 19310
Phone: (610) 593-1777
FAX: (610) 593-2002
E-mail: Schifferbk@aol.com.
Visit our web site at: www.schifferbooks.com
Please write for a free catalog.
This book may be purchased from the publisher.
Please include $3.95 postage.
Try your bookstore first.

In Europe, Schiffer books are distributed by:
Bushwood Books
6 Marksbury Ave.
Kew Gardens
Surrey TW9 4JF
England
Phone: 44 (0)208 392-8585
FAX: 44 (0)208 392-9876
E-mail: Bushwd@aol.com.
Free postage in the UK. Europe: air mail at cost.
Try your bookstore first.

INTRODUCTION

The original water-colors and oil panels here reproduced are from the Anne S.K. Brown Military Collection at Brown University Library in Providence, Rhode Island, one of the largest repositories of illustrations and documentation of the uniforms of the world from earliest times up to the present day. These particular images were acquired by Mrs. John Nicholas Brown from Francis Edwards Ltd. of London in 1966 and the full set consists of 61 tempera drawings on board by John McNeill, 89 signed water-colors by William Barnes Wollen, Ernest Ibbetson and Edgar A. Holloway, an additional 49 water-colors by Ibbetson, and 66 oil paintings on board by Henry ("Harry") Payne. All were commissioned by the famous publishing company of Gale and Polden Ltd. of Aldershot, Hampshire, England, to be issued as uniform postcards under the titles of *History & Traditions* and *Regimental uniforms*, although some were used also by the company in their various military books and short regimental histories[1]. Sometimes the same picture was used in different series; for instance, McNeill's painting of the Royal Scots appears in the *History & Traditions* series, as a card surrounded by a tartan border; and as a card with no border. A handful of small narrow boards painted by McNeill were commissioned by G. Falkner & Sons of Manchester and London for a series of postcards depicting single figures and the regimental crest.

In the late 1860s, T. Ernest Polden went into partnership with his mentor, James Gale, and established a business in Old Brompton near Chatham, Kent. By the 1890s they had opened a branch office in the famous army town of Aldershot, with other branches in Portsmouth and London. Being close to the center of army and naval activity in Aldershot and Portsmouth respectively enabled Gale & Polden to obtain commissions to publish training manuals and other Service publications. The *Military Mail*, a weekly journal was started by the company in 1901 and ran until 1914; and in 1902 the first postcards were published. They ranged from views of military places, military history and traditions, military badges, and the famous sets depicting regimental uniforms. These publications continued throughout the Great War and included recruiting cards and silk cards prepared in France for sale at home. Despite the destruction of the Aldershot factory by fire in 1918, Gale & Polden continued to produce military books over the next few decades.

Their catalogues appeared frequently with images of their premises at Amen Corner, London, Nelson House, Portsmouth and their headquarters at the Wellington Works, Aldershot, reproduced on the back cover. The company described itself as 'military printers, publishers and photographers'. During the Second World War, they produced considerable work for the British army and government so much so that they made large profits. But as army work lessened, they had to diversify. In order to achieve this they installed new equipment capable of producing works like 'The Queen' very quickly.[2] Unfortunately, the large orders required to sustain the investment did not appear and by 1965 the venerable firm had to close down; its last postcard series had appeared in 1959. All materials and resources disappeared in no time and thus the original designs for the postcards were dispersed. More was thrown away so this collection of original pictures is a rare survival.

The Artists

The artists of these fine, exquisite paintings were all leading military illustrators at the beginning of the twentieth century. For the *History and Traditions* series which received the official sanction of the army, the artists selected were John McNeill and Ernest Ibbetson, and their paintings date from between 1908 and 1916. While both painted infantry figures, Ibbetson was responsible for painting the cavalry regiments as well.

McNeill, born in 1872, had a short military career as a private in the Lancashire Fusiliers; his record reads as follows: 3477 Cpl J. McNeill enlisted at Bury on 28/10/1890 aged 18 1/2. Fresh complexion, Brown Eyes, Brown Hair, 5' 5 1/2" tall, Chest 32", Weight 111 lbs. He was born in Manchester, a laborer by trade and a Roman Catholic."[3] Apparently he deserted on 24 January 1891 and re-enlisted later that year on the 27 October. His record states that he was discharged on 10 August 1903, his character being listed as

'Very Good.' According to Greenwall, McNeill was present at the battle of Omdurman and in the Boer War at Spion Kop. A picture in the Bury museum dating from the war depicts 'Corporal Skinner, Blockhouse, Tvl [Transvaal] 1901'. Besides providing illustrations for Gale & Polden, he also created designs for the Falkner series of military cards. His water-colors for the Gale & Polden series all bear the date 1908.

Ernest Ibbetson was born in Yorkshire in 1877 and studied art in various local towns and in Paris.[4] Following his training, he became a free-lance illustrator although he always had a passion for the military and in 1896 joined the Artist's Rifles. He volunteered for the Boer War and served in both world wars. He died in 1959. Ibbetson was a prolific illustrator and his work appeared in various publications including the *Penny Illustrated Paper* for which he worked during the Boer War. Ibbetson was still producing water-colors for Gale & Polden postcard series into the 1940s and 1950s.

Edgar A. Holloway (not to be confused with the Yorkshire-born artist of the same name born in 1914), was a military illustrator known today primarily through his work for Gale & Polden. One of his projects was the 'Wellington Series' of postcards depicting foreign kings in the uniforms of colonels in chiefs of various British regiments. Besides providing illustrations for postcards, he also supplied pictures for reproduction in the short regimental histories published by the company. His illustrations appeared in various newspapers such as *The Regiment*, *Shurey's Illustrated*, and *Shurey's Pictorial Budget*, and he illustrated various military books including *Christians in Khaki* (1900) and *Old Fireproof: behind the Chaplain's Story* (1912).[5]

Of all the artists represented, Harry Payne was the most significant. In Gale & Polden's early catalogues, he is the only artist identified in the postcard listings; others are listed simply as 'well-known artists', although by the 1940s, they were listing Ernest Ibbetson by name. In the 1921 catalogue, the caption under the entry for 'Post Cards of the Uniforms of the British Army' reads: 'Illustrating the Uniforms of the present day, beautifully reproduced in Colours from the Original Oil Paintings by the well-known military artist, Harry Payne.' Henry Joseph (or Harry) Payne was born in 1858 and died in 1927. He was a volunteer with the West Kent Yeomanry, but was a professional artist producing numerous paintings for book illustrations, commercial prints, and postcards.[6]

William Barnes Wollen's five water-colors are not reproduced in the present work. Born in 1857, he was a significant academic painter of military scenes and battles in the late Victorian and early twentieth century and many of his canvases were exhibited at the Royal Academy.[7] He also served as a special artist for *The Sphere* during the South African War. He produced a large quantity of illustrations for books, postcards and other military publications. The artist died in 1936.

How the pictures were produced.

John McNeill's intricate tempera paintings were done on Whatman's Water Colour Sketching Boards sold by Winsor & Newton. The boards are cut in half and on the verso is the title of each regiment written in McNeill's hand, along with a penciled number relating to Gale & Polden memorandums (see below). The paintings measure approximately 16 x 12 cm. and usually occupy the left side of the board, the right side being unpainted but marking the area where the battle honors, history and traditions and nicknames of each regiment would be printed. The pictures are squared off with pencil lines and occasionally have measurements noted or writing such as 'to match historical cards'. Sometimes, the rough edges of the water-colors are covered by white tape; while on some, an extra piece of board has been affixed to allow the picture to be more vertical. Along the edges of the boards are pinholes to fasten the board down either by the artist or the printer, and some of the boards have a paper covering flap to protect the water-colors.

Smaller postcard-size paintings on quarter-size board with the regimental crest painted above the figures and the title painted below were produced for Falkner & Sons. None of the pictures are dated although all are signed by McNeill. One water-color of the King's Royal Rifle Corps has pencil notations as follows:

'do not make edges of green background or foreground too harsh'.

And at the bottom of the card:

'figure & background only required no title or badge'.

Ibbetson's pictures were painted between 1909 and 1916 for the *History & Traditions* series, of which there were 146 cards. Some bear the date 1909 while one is dated 1910. On the verso of two are the dates 'January 18, 1916', and 'March 15, 1916'. Several have pencil notations near the image giving directions and details of the uniforms. Ibbetson painted groups of six pictures for the various infantry regiments and some of these included scenes from the Great War. He also painted cavalry in full dress uniforms. Painted on board, Ibbetson's pictures measure approximately 34 x 22 cm. The resulting postcards bore a color picture of uniformed figures on the left side, whilst on the right was the regimental badge, battle honors, and a paragraph describing the history and tradition of the particular regiment as with the McNeill series.

By 1908, the final version of the full dress uniform was being worn by the British Army and it was this uniform which Gale & Polden wished to reproduce as postcards. It is not known how the artists went about their work but as the company was headquartered in Aldershot and the project had been authorized by the War Office, it is quite probable that McNeill and Ibbetson had access to the regimental clothing depot and may have had soldiers to model the uniforms for them. According to McGuirl, the water-colors were forwarded to the adjutants or Regimental Sergeant Majors of the various regiments for comments, corrections or alterations. Each picture usually contained two figures of different rank sometimes facing each other. Some pairings were in full dress while others contrasted full dress with either walking-out dress or drill order. McNeill in particular paid special attention to detail and his fine, intricate representation of campaign medals and collar badges on the tunics of various figures shows the care he took in every painting. His figures represent Infantry of the Line, artillery or services, while Ibbetson's depicts infantry, services and cavalry.

Edgar Holloway painted his scenes during the first two years of the Great War, each on Whatman boards measuring 33 x 22 cm. They were painted in groups of six pictures per regiment for the Gale & Polden *Alphabet* series. For instance, the six water-colors depicting the Royal Scots include such titles as "Showing his Paces," "Defending a Village," and "A Topping Story." Holloway's pieces are particularly informative as to how the pictures were created and their attempt at accuracy. Like some of the Ibbetson pictures, there are occasional pencil notations but it is on the verso where the most revealing details are found. Pencil notations on many of the boards for all the artists sometimes have the words of approval by the publisher: 'Correct', 'OK' or 'Passed by...'; others have a reference number which relates to Gale & Polden memoranda which were often attached to the pictures. While many of these were removed later, some have survived on the verso of Holloway's pictures. In the series depicting the Northumberland Fusiliers, for example, are several memorandum which reveal the process and the exchange of communications between artist and publisher. On the verso of Number 4 is the following:

Memorandum from Gale & Polden, Ltd., Wellington Works, Aldershot. [number]To Amen Corner, 6 Dec. 1915 [date stamped]. The rear officer seems turning into an impossible angle with his body to keep the seat.

On the verso of *Number 2 Northumberland Fusiliers. The celebrated third colour, St. George's Day'* appear the following labels:

Memorandum from Gale & Polden, Ltd., Wellington Works, Aldershot. To Amen Corner, 21/12/15. Northumberland Fusiliers. The celebrated third colour. Correct. Drum majors [sic] sash we find is worn by many regiments as you say over the shoulder strap.

Below this is another sheet pasted on:

Buglers [sic] wings on shoulders should stand out square with shoulder also the Drum Major [small pencil sketch]. Drum

Major should have sash under shoulder strap. Also sash at top (next collar) is too high up to look well. South African Ribbon is minus its blue stripes & we note Drum Major has the Egyptian Medals of 84 we think which makes him rather a boy that period. Gold lace on his collar. We have no record of the red belt of Drum Major.

Holloway responded in a pencil notation to the question about the sash under shoulder strap:

'If this means the sash over left shoulder I fancy you will find this remark, as I have a photo of the Drum Major showing the sash over the shoulder strap. This appears to be usual - see your W. Yorkshire Regt. Drum Major. Also your Post Card No. 50 (East Yorkshire Regt. 15th Foot).

Pencil reply to note about red belt:

"I was given to understand it was, but am now told it is brown leather. EAH"

On the verso of *No. 5 Northumberland Fusiliers. Outside the Guard Room* are two labels and some pencil notations:

Memorandum from Gale & Polden, Ltd., Wellington Works, Aldershot. To Amen Corner, 6 Dec. 1915 [Date stamped]. Re Holloways Northumberland Fusiliers. No. 5 Outside the Guard Room. This is correct as far as pencil out[line] shows we cannot quite grasp the *"topography" of the Guard Room* but no doubt Mr. Holloway is working... [piece missing].

Below in pencil notation initialed by Holloway:

On the pencil sketch. Aldershot post? "Porch". Guard rooms with Porches may be seen at Wellington Barracks, London. Hounslow. Plymouth, & many other garrison towns.

EHA

Another small label is attached below this notation which reads:

Northumberland Fusiliers outside Guard Room. We quite agree to "porch" guardroom, in the rough. We could not quite grasp what was meant as shadows were confusing.

On the verso of *No. 5 Northumberland Fusiliers "A New Trophy"* is the pencil notation 'Now quite correct."

The latest group of pictures are those by Harry Payne painted for Gale & Polden between 1918 and 1920.[8] There are a total of 67 panels painted in oil on 'Academy Board for Oil Painting (Granulated Surface)' manufactured by Reeves & Sons, London. Apparently only 22 were produced as postcards in 11 sets. As with the other artists, Payne depicted the two members of various regiments in full dress. While all the pictures bear Payne's usual signature, none are dated. One has a Gale & Polden label attached bearing their address and dated 4/2/20; while many show evidence of having had a sheet of white paper (probably a Gale & Polden memorandum) attached but later removed leaving an edge. The pictures are titled in pencil and sometimes have a label on the verso with the title of the regiment, or the title painted in white ink.

Sometimes Payne used old paintings to provide board for his uniform pictures on the blank side. One has a portrait study of a lady, while another appears to have a self-portrait of the artist in the uniform of the West Kent Yeomanry, and a horse. A large water-color painting of two troopers of the 16th Lancers in the field signed by signed by Payne, has been cut in half and two uniform panels painted on the reverse sides.

All the postcard series went through several printings and varying titles and as late as 1949 Gale & Polden were writing from the Wellington Press, Aldershot, to Anne S.K. Brown in Washington, D.C. offering sets of postcards entitled 'McNeill's Series', '19 kinds at 2d each', and 'Payne's Series', '15 kinds at 2d each'. The company did note that "we are unable to offer you complete sets of the various series as many of the Units are now out of print and will not be reprinted." They were also offering their 'new series of Service Post Cards' from original sketches by Ibbetson. Today, Gale & Polden's military postcards attract a large following of collectors, and postcards that once sold for two pennies a card can now fetch several pounds a card if they can be found on the open market.

References

Byatt, Anthony. *Picture Postcards and their Publishers* (Malvern, 1978)

Cane, Michael. *Harry Payne* (London, 1972)

Harris, R. G. Harry Payne - Military Artist', *Tradition* No. 46 (1970), 13-16

McGuirl, Thomas, 'Old Military Postcards', *Military Modelling* (March 1987), 196-198

Sammons, Jack, 'A Force to be Reckoned With. Military Postcards by Jack Sammons', *Military Chest*, Vol. 2, No. 5 (September-October 1983), 44

Sammons, Jack, 'The Gale & Polden Story. Military Postcards by Jack Sammons', *Military Chest*, Vol. 5, No. 4 (September-October 1986), 26-27

Notes

[1] For example, see *Regimental Nicknames and Traditions of the British Army* (1915) containing pictures by Wollen, Holloway and Ibbetson; and *A Short History of the Warwickshire Regiment* (1921) which reproduces one of the McNeill panels.

[2] Information on Gale & Polden during and after World War II has been supplied by William Y. Carman.

[3] McNeill's service record which is in the Lancashire Headquarters of the Royal Regiment of Fusiliers at Bury, Lancashire, is quoted in Ryno Greenwall, *Artists & Illustrators of the Boer War* (1992), 171. Greenwall reproduces two humorous water-colors by McNeill; one, dated 1902 and entitled 'Modern Tactics' shows a kilted soldier supporting a large boulder on his shoulders; the second, 'How we took Pieters Hill' depicts two figures, a soldier in blue overalls and one dressed as a priest.

[4] I am grateful to Dr. F.A. Barrett of York University, Toronto, for details about Ibbetson's life.

[5] Greenwall, *op. cit.*, 149.

[6] Details on Payne's life are drawn from Michael Cane, *For Queen and Country. The Career of Harry Payne, Military Artist, 1858-1927* (Kingston, Surrey, Michael Cane), 1977, pages 65-67.

[7] For further details and reproductions of some of Wollen's paintings see Peter Harrington, *British Artists and War: The Face of Battle in Paintings and Prints 1700-1914* (London, Greenhill, 1993).

[8] Cane, op. cit., 65-67.

THE PLATES

John McNeill - **Highland Light Infantry**

John McNeill - **Black Watch (Royal Highlanders)**

John McNeill - **Queen's Own Cameron Highlanders**

John McNeill - **Devonshire Regiment**

John McNeill - **The Royal Fusiliers**

John McNeill - **Connaught Rangers**

John McNeill - **Essex Regiment**

John McNeill - **South Lancashire Regiment**

John McNeill - **The Oxfordshire & Buckinghamshire Light Infantry**

John McNeill - **Royal Sussex Regiment**

John McNeill - **Hampshire Regiment**

John McNeill - **Princess Victoria's (Royal Irish Fusiliers)**

John McNeill - **The Manchester Regiment**

John McNeill - **The Duke of Edinburgh's (Wiltshire Regiment)**

John McNeill - **The Gloustershire Regiment**

John McNeill - **The Norfolk Regiment**

John McNeill - **The Prince Albert's (Somerset Light Infantry)**

John McNeill - **Bedfordshire Regiment**

John McNeill - **Royal Warwickshire Regiment**

John McNeill - **Royal Welsh Fusiliers**

John McNeill - **Dorsetshire Regiment**

John McNeill - **South Wales Borderers**

John McNeill - **King's (Liverpool) Regiment**

John McNeill - **The Queen's (Royal West Surrey Regiment)**

John McNeill - **King's Own Scottish Borderer's**

John McNeill - **Royal Munster Fusiliers**

John McNeill - **Northamptonshire Regiment**

John McNeill - **Suffolk Regiment**

John McNeill - **The Royal Inniskilling Fusiliers**

John McNeill - **Worcestershire Regiment**

John McNeill - **Lancashire Fusiliers**

John McNeill - **Prince of Wales's Leinster Regiment**

John McNeill - **Loyal North Lancashire Regiment**

John McNeill - **Rifle Brigade**

John McNeill - **Cameronians (Scottish Rifles)**

John McNeill - **The Royal Dublin Fusiliers**

THE LINCOLNSHIRE REGIMENT.

John McNeill - **Lincolnshire Regiment**

THE PRINCE OF WALES'S OWN
(WEST YORKSHIRE REGIMENT.)

John McNeill - **Prince of Wales's Own (West Yorkshire Regiment)**

Copyright.

EAST YORKSHIRE REGIMENT

John McNeill - **East Yorkshire Regiment**

QUIS SEPARABIT

G. Falkner & Sons
Manchester & London.

RIFLEMAN
MOUNTED INFANTRY COMPANY
FIELD SERVICE ORDER

THE ROYAL IRISH RIFLES.

John McNeill - **Royal Irish Rifles**

John McNeill - **Duke of Wellington's West Riding Regiment**

THE DURHAM LIGHT INFANTRY.

John McNeill - **Durham Light Infantry**

CEDE NULLIS

THE KING'S OWN (YORKSHIRE LIGHT INFANTRY)

John McNeill - **King's Own (Yorkshire Light Infantry)**

THE YORK AND LANCASTER REGIMENT.

John McNeill - **York and Lancaster Regiment**

THE SHERWOOD FORESTERS
(NOTTINGHAMSHIRE & DERBYSHIRE REGIMENT)

John McNeill - **Sherwood Foresters (Nottingham & Derbyshire Regiment)**

John McNeill - **Queen's Own (Royal West Kent Regiment)**

John McNeill - **Duke of Cambridge's Own (Middlesex Regiment)**

John McNeill - **The King's (Shropshire Light Infantry)**

John McNeill - **The Buffs (East Kent Regiment)**

John McNeill - **Cheshire Regiment**

John McNeill - **Welsh Regiment**

John McNeill - **Princess Charlotte of Wales's (Royal Berkshire Regiment)**

John McNeill - **Princess Louise's (Argyll & Sutherland Highlanders)**

John McNeill - **Seaforth Highlanders (Ross-Shire Buffs, The Duke of Albany's)**

John McNeill - **East Surrey Regiment**

John McNeill - **Royal Irish Regiment**

John McNeill - **Duke of Cornwall's Light Infantry**

John McNeill - **Royal Army Medical Corps**

John McNeill - **East Lancashire Regiment**

MINDEN DAY

John McNeill - **Northumberland Fusiliers**

John McNeill - **King's Royal Rifle Corps**

Ernest Ibbetson - **1st Life Guards**

Ernest Ibbetson - **2nd Life Guards**

Ernest Ibbetson - **Lincolnshire Regiment**

Ernest Ibbetson - **Northumberland Fusiliers**

Ernest Ibbetson - **Welsh Guards (Drill Order)**

Ernest Ibbetson - **South Wales Borderers (The Colours No.2)**

Ernest Ibbetson - **South Wales Borderers (The Company Commander No.3)**

Ernest Ibbetson - **The Lancashire Fusiliers (The C.O. [Marching Past] No.4)**

Ernest Ibbetson - **Prince of Wales's Own West Yorkshire Regiment (The Colors No.2)**

Ernest Ibbetson - **Prince of Wales's Own West Yorkshire Regiment (The Drum Major No.2)**

Ernest Ibbetson - **Prince of Wales's Own West Yorkshire Regiment (The C.O. [Battalion Marching Past])**

Ernest Ibbetson - **Yorkshire Regiment (marching Past No.4)**

Ernest Ibbetson - **Yorkshire Regiment (Unfix Bayonets No.2)**

Ernest Ibbetson - **Yorkshire Regiment**

Ernest Ibbetson - **The Royal Fusiliers (Captain, Undress and Regiment Sergeant Major [Guard Mounting Inspection])**

Ernest Ibbetson - **The Royal Fusiliers (The C.O.)**

Ernest Ibbetson - **The Royal Fusiliers**

Ernest Ibbetson - **7th (Princess Royal's) Dragoon Guards**

Ernest Ibbetson - **3rd Dragoon Guards**

Ernest Ibbetson - **1st (Royal) Dragoons**

Ernest Ibbetson - **5th (Royal Irish) Lancers**

Ernest Ibbetson - **3rd (King's) Hussars**

Ernest Ibbetson - **14th (King's) Hussars**

Ernest Ibbetson - **Military Mounted Police**

Ernest Ibbetson - **Sherwood Foresters (Fixing Bayonets! No.5)**

Ernest Ibbetson - **Gloustershire Regiment (The C.O./Battalion marching Past No.3)**

Edgar A. Holloway - **No.2 Northumberland Fusiliers (The Celebrated Third Colour, St. George's Day)**

Edgar A. Holloway - **No.4 Northumberland Fusiliers (Colonel and Adjutant)**

Edgar A. Holloway - **No.5 Northumberland Fusiliers (Outside the Guard Room)**

Edgar A. Holloway - **No.1 Worcestershire Regiment (The Colours)**

Edgar A. Holloway - **No.2 Worcestershire Regiment (Battalion Marching out of Barracks)**

Edgar A. Holloway - **No.3 Worcestershire Regiment (The Guard Room)**

Edgar A. Holloway - **No.4 Worcestershire Regiment (Captain and Adjutant and Lieutenant)**

Edgar A. Holloway - **No.2 Cheshire Regiment (For Valour)**

Edgar A. Holloway - **No.3 Cheshire Regiment (The Colours)**

Edgar A. Holloway - **No.4 Cheshire Regiment (A Levée)**

Edgar A. Holloway - **No.6 Cheshire Regiment (Drum Major and Drums)**

Edgar A. Holloway - **No.1 Royal Scots (Showing his Paces)**

Edgar A. Holloway - **No.3 Royal Scots**

Edgar A. Holloway - **No.5 Royal Scots (A Topping Story)**

Edgar A. Holloway - **No.6 Royal Scots (Pipe Major)**

Edgar A. Holloway - **No.1 King's (Liverpool Regiment) (Presenting New Colours)**

Edgar A. Holloway - **No.3 The King's (Liverpool Regiment) (Our Captain and Adjutant)**

Edgar A. Holloway - **No.4 The King's (Liverpool Regiment) (Undress, Full and Mess)**

Edgar A. Holloway - **No.5 The King's (Liverpool Regiment) (Relieving Sentry)**

Edgar A. Holloway - **No.1 Royal Highlanders (Black Watch)**

Edgar A. Holloway - **No.2 Royal Highlanders (Black Watch)**

Edgar A. Holloway - **No.3 Royal Highlanders (Black Watch)**

Edgar A. Holloway - **No.4 Royal Highlanders (Black Watch) (Spoils of Victory, 1916)**

Edgar A. Holloway - **No.5 Royal Highlanders (Colonel and Bugler)**

Edgar A. Holloway - **No.6 Royal Highlanders (Drill Orders)**

Edgar A. Holloway - **No.1 The Welsh Regiment**

Edgar A. Holloway - **No.2 The Welsh Regiment**

Edgar A. Holloway - **No.4 The Welsh Regiment ("Billy" The Regimental Pet)**

Edgar A. Holloway - **No.5 The Welsh Regiment (Captain and Adjutant)**

Henry ("Harry") Payne - **The Royal Dublin Fusiliers (102nd and 103rd Foot)**

Henry ("Harry") Payne - **The Hampshire Regiment (37th and 67th Foot)**

Henry ("Harry") Payne - **Prince of Wales Leinster Regiment (Royal Canadians) (100th and 109th Foot)**

Henry ("Harry") Payne - **The Bedfordshire Regiment (16th Foot)**

Henry ("Harry") Payne - **The Lincolnshire Regiment 910th Foot)**

Henry ("Harry") Payne - **Prince of Wales North Staffordshire Regiment (64th Foot)**

Henry ("Harry") Payne - **The Loyal North Lancashire Regiment (80th Foot)**

Henry ("Harry") Payne - **The Cheshire Regiment (22nd Foot)**

Henry ("Harry") Payne - **The Royal Fusiliers (7th Foot)**

Henry ("Harry") Payne - **King's Own Yorkshire Light Infantry (51st and 105th Foot)**

Henry ("Harry") Payne - **Royal Scots Fusiliers (21st Foot)**

Henry ("Harry") Payne - **The Duke of Wellington's West Riding Regiment**

Henry ("Harry") Payne - **The South Wales Borderers (24th Foot)**

Henry ("Harry") Payne - **The York and Lancaster Regiment (65th and 84th Foot)**

Henry ("Harry") Payne - **Royal Irish Fusiliers (87th and 89th Foot)**

Henry ("Harry") Payne - **The Connaught Rangers (88th and 94th Foot)**

Henry ("Harry") Payne - **Royal Irish Rifles (83rd and 86th Foot)**

Henry ("Harry") Payne - **The Manchester Regiment (63rd and 96th Foot)**

Henry ("Harry") Payne - **East Lancashire Regiment (30th and 59th Foot)**

Henry ("Harry") Payne - **The Queen's Royal West Surrey Regiment (2nd Foot)**

Henry ("Harry") Payne - **Royal Munster Fusiliers (101st and 104th Foot)**

Also from the Publisher

Art of the Flight Jacket: Classic Leather Jackets of World War II. Jon A. Maguire & John P. Conway. Following the success of their first volume *American Flight Jackets, Airmen & Aircraft: A History of U.S. Flyers' Jackets from World War I to Desert Storm*, Jon Maguire and John Conway focus solely on the painted leather jackets of the World War II years in this all new volume.
Size: 8 1/2" x 11" • over 600 color and b/w photos • 176 pp.
ISBN: 0-88740-794-3 • hard cover • $49.95

Gear Up! Flight Clothing & Equipment of USAAF Airmen in WWII. Jon A. Maguire. Provides an in-depth examination of personal flight clothing and equipment used by United States Army Air Force flyers in World War II. In addition to U.S. issue items, the book also covers RAF gear used by American airmen. The original items are presented in full color photographs, including detail shots and labels. Also included are hundreds of World War II era photographs showing the items in use, as they were worn. Portions of actual USAAF instructional manuals are provided as well. A valuable reference to historians, collectors, and modelers.
Size: 8 1/2" x 11" • over 600 b/w and color photos • 184 pp.
ISBN: 0-88740-744-7 • hard cover • $45.00

Spalding Aviator's Clothing and Equipment in the 1920s-1930s. This facsimile reprint covers the variety of flying clothing and equipment manufactured by Spalding during the 1920s and 1930s, including flying suits, leather jackets, helmets, face masks, oxygen helmets, gloves and gauntlets, women's flying suits, jackets and coats, leather coats, waders, boots, goggles, and parachutes.
Size: 6" x 9" • over 130 b/w images • 36 pp.
ISBN: 0-7643-0403-8 • soft cover • $9.95

Silver Wings, Pinks & Greens: Uniforms, Wings & Insignia of USAAF Airmen in WWII. Jon A. Maguire. This new look at the uniforms and insignia of the USAAF during the World War II years covers a broad range of clothing, collar insignia, rank insignia, shoulder/sleeve insignia and squadron patches. Additionally, there is an in-depth examination of wing qualification badges. Actual items are presented in nearly 600 illustrations in full color, and also as they appeared in actual war-era photos. Actual uniform regulations and illustrations from the 1943 and 1944 Officer's Guides are also provided.
Size: 8 1/2" x 11" • over 500 b/w and color photos • 192 pp.
ISBN: 0-88740-578-9 • hard cover • $45.00

More Silver Wings, Pinks & Greens: An Expanded Study of USAS, USAAC, & USAAF Uniforms, Wings & Insignia • 1913-1945 Including Civilian Auxiliaries. Jon A. Maguire. All new material that greatly expands on the items presented in the first book. Additionally, this work covers totally new areas including Civil Air Patrol, W.A.S.P.s, Air Transport Command, Factory Techincal Representatives, and "Yanks" in the RAF and RCAF. Also included are uniforms and insignia of the First World War era, and the "Golden Age" of the 1920s-1930s. There is also a large section on Aviation Cadets and civilian contract flying schools and instructors. Includes period photographs showing the items as they were worn.
Size: 8 1/2" x 11" • over 1,100 color and b/w photos • 350 pp.
ISBN: 0-7643-0091-1 • hard cover • $79.95

Luftwaffe vs. RAF: Flying Clothing of the Air War, 1939-45. Mick J. Prodger. An up-close and serious examination of the various patterns of flight jackets, suits, headgear and gloves worn by the courageous pilots and aircrews of these two great adversaries during WWII. This book includes a look at some of the more bizarre and experimental outfits as well as the standard flying kit for different climates and regions, with a special section on electrically-heated clothing. Also examined is the parallel development of flying clothing in the Luftwaffe and the Royal Air Force, and the surprising influence each country had upon the other. An invaluable reference source for collectors, re-enactors, artists, modellers, and historians.
Size: 9" x 12" • over 500 color and b/w photographs • 160 pp.
ISBN: 0-7643-0234-5 • hard cover • $49.95

Luftwaffe vs. RAF: Flying Equipment of the Air War, 1939-45. Mick J. Prodger. This second of a two volume study closely examines the development and uses of personal flying equipment of the Luftwaffe and RAF throughout WWII. From compasses secreted in tunic buttons, to floating rations, to suits with built-in parachutes, you'll find it all. All types of parachutes and harnesses, life preservers, inflatable boats, survival tools, weapons for self-defense, and even some of the paperwork and personal items carried by the airmen of these two opposing air forces. Study the sophisticated rescue and survival equipment available to Luftwaffe crews, alongside the clever, yet often brilliantly simple devices which enabled so many RAF flyers to evade capture.
Size: 9" x 12" • over 500 color and b/w photographs • 144 pp.
ISBN: 0-7643-0249-3 • hard cover • $49.95

Head Dress of the British Heavy Cavalry: 1842-1934. David JJ Rowe. Here is a book dedicated to the head-dress worn by the British Heavy Cavalry of the period 1842 to the present day. It is lavishly illustrated with both colour and black and white photographs of helmets, most of which have never previously been published.

This book is an essential source of reference for both the established, and new collectors, and to the student of cavalry full dress uniforms of the period 1842-1934.
Size: 9" x 12" • 135 color and b/w photographs • 256 pp.
ISBN: 0-7643-0957-9 • hard cover • $75.00

Eagles Recalled: Pilot and Aircrew Wings of Canada, Great Britain and the British Commonwealth 1913-1945. Warren Carroll. These pieces of cloth and metal symbolize the daring, bravery, suffering and loss of men who flew in deadly aerial battles for democratic freedom. Much of the material contained in this publication has never been published. The author has also made new historical discoveries presented here for the very first time – he has accessed private collections, photographed rare museum acquisitions, and received support from historians in seven countries over a period of some ten years. This work brings to readers a detailed and comprehensive study of the brevets issued to aviators who fought with Great Britain in World Wars I and II.
Size: 8 1/2" x 11" • over 800 color and b/w photos • 240 pp.
ISBN: 0-7643-0244-2 • hard cover • $79.95

Vintage Flying Helmets: Aviation Headgear before the Jet Age. Mick J. Prodger. This new book explores the history and development of early flying headgear throughout the pioneering nations in military and sport aviation, from the earliest exploits of the Wright Brothers, to the end of World War II. Drawn from aviation museums and private collections from around the world, the illustrated color section features over 1000 photographs depicting more than 650 different items of flying headgear: helmets, goggles, oxygen masks and accessories, including many unique personalizations and rarely seen items.
Size: 9" x 12" • over 1,000 color and b/w photographs • 336 pp.
ISBN: 0-88740-776-5 • hard cover • $75.00

Jet Age Flight Helmets: Aviation Headgear in the Modern Age. Alan R. Wise & Michael S. Breuninger. This is the first book ever to cover in detail the history and development of military flight helmets from the post-World War II era to the present, and includes over 120 different helmets and their associated equipment such as oxygen masks, boom microphones, inner helmets etc. Specific details of each helmet include manufacturer, proper designation, unique features, accessories, periods of use, branch of service(s), and aircraft in which is was used-selected export users are also included.
Size: 9" x 12" • over 1,000 color and b/w photographs • 248 pp.
ISBN: 0-7643-0070-9 • hard cover • $75.00

Pilots' Information File 1944: The Authentic World War II Guidebook for Pilots and Flight Engineers. The Pilots' Information File (PIF) was the standard reference for any general information required of USAAF pilots and flight engineers. The PIF covered items of a general nature that a combat flyer must know in order to fight an air war and survive.
Size: 8 1/2" x 11" • photographs, drawings, diagrams • 268 pp.
ISBN: 0-88740-780-3 • soft cover • $19.95

The M-1 Helmet: A History of the U.S. M-1 Helmet in World War II. Mark A. Reynosa. Presents over seven years of research into the history of the M-1 helmet during World War II, and provides the most comprehensive examination of its development and production. All aspects of M-1 helmet production are covered including: the helmet body, the fiber liner, the plastic liner, the parachutist helmet, helmet camouflage, helmet modifications, helmet paint schemes, and toy helmets. Every production helmet version is presented in full color photographs, including detail shots and production markings. Also included are World War II era photographs of the helmet samples, helmet production, and helmets worn in training or in action. This book is a valuable reference to both historians and collectors.
Size: 8 1/2" x 11" • over 350 color and b/w photos • 112 pp.
ISBN: 0-7643-0074-1 • hard cover • $39.95

Post-World War II M-1 Helmets: An Illustrated Study. Mark A. Reynosa. This book presents several years of research into the history of America's post-World War II M-1 Helmet. It provides the most comprehensive look into the research, development, and production of the M-1 Helmet during this often overlooked period. All aspects of the M-1 Helmet are covered, as well as associated research and development programs that impacted the helmet, such as the Nylon Helmet Program. Included are contract sheets, contract number reference, military specification drawings, and photos of helmet samples and production.
Size: 8 1/2" x 11" • over 260 color and b/w photos • 136 pp.
ISBN: 0-7643-1033-X • hard cover • $39.95

U.S. Combat Helmets of the 20th Century: Mass Production Helmets. Mark A. Reynosa. This book represents nearly a decade of research into the history of U.S. production combat helmets. Covered are the standard ground helmets, parachutist helmets and helmet covers. Every major production helmet version is presented in full color photographs, including detail shots and production markings.
Size: 8 1/2" x 11" • over 250 color and b/w photos • 112 pp.
ISBN: 0-7643-0357-0 • hard cover • $39.95

The Personnel Armor System Ground Troops (PASGT) Helmet: An Illustrated Study of the U.S. Military's Current Issue Helmet. Mark A. Reynosa. This book presents the history of the U.S. military's current issue helmet – the PASGT ("passget") Helmet - and provides the most comprehensive look into the research, development, and production of the helmet between 1971 and the present. All aspects of the PASGT Helmet are covered, including the early research and development efforts that resulted in the final helmet design and construction. The book supplements coverage of this early period with photographs of the various helmets. Also included are contract sheets and military specification drawings.
Size: 8 1/2" x 11" • over 115 color and b/w photos • 80 pp.
ISBN: 0-7643-1034-8 • soft cover • $19.95

Geronimo! U.S. Airborne Uniforms, Insignia & Equipment in World War II. Bill Rentz. This book explores the uniforms, insignia, and equipment of American Airborne, Glider, Troop Carrier, and Airborne Engineers in World War II. Detailed, up-close images of individual items, multi-side views of full combat rig, and over 100 World War II era photos, most unpublished, showing the uniforms and equipment as worn by the troops. Included is a comparative section with both British and German airborne gear. A detailed look at the clothing and equipment of America's Finest, and an important reference work for the airborne collector, reenactor, historian and veteran.
Size: 9" x 12" • over 630 color and b/w photographs • 192 pp.
ISBN: 0-7643-0677-4 • hard cover • $59.95

For King and Country: British Airborne Uniforms, Insignia & Equipment in World War II • 1st Airborne Division • 6th Airborne Division • 1st Polish Independent Parachute Brigade. Harlan Glenn. The first in a series of in-depth studies which will cover the uniforms, equipment, insignia, weapons, vehicles, and personal items of the British and Commonwealth soldier of World War II. This initial volume covers the British Airborne soldier of the 1st and 6th Airborne Divisions, and the 1st Polish Independent Parachute Brigade. An essential reference for any military enthusiast, collector, reenactor, and modeler.
Size: 9" x 12" • over 600 color and b/w photographs • 192 pp.
ISBN: 0-7643-0794-0 • hard cover • $59.95

German Paratroops: Uniforms, Insignia & Equipment of the Fallschirmjäger in World War II. Robert Kurtz. The uniforms and equipment of the elite German Fallschirmjäger is the subject of this detailed, illustrated study. Authentic items - smocks, dress tunics, boots, insignia, helmets, visor caps, gloves, knee pads and more - are shown in superb color photos, in both multiple full-view, and detail shots. Unpublished World War II era photos show uniforms and equipment being worn on a variety of war fronts. Also included is a short chapter covering other Axis airborne including Italian and Japanese gear.
Size: 9" x 12" • over 530 color and b/w photographs • 200 pp.
ISBN: 0-7643-1040-2 • hard cover • $59.95

U.S. Chemical and Biological Defense Respirators: An Illustrated History. Chris Carey. A historical overview of United States military and civilian defense respirator developments from the beginnings of CBW respiratory protection in the First World War. Accompanied by photographs, illustrations and other supplemental material, the book serves as a valuable reference for military historians, NBC defense specialists concerned with the design, development and evolution of military and civil individual protection against war agents, and even collectors of military memorabilia. Provides an informational starting point for individuals interested in developing personal understanding about a relatively exotic and important area of modern defensive technology.
Size: 8 1/2" x 11" • over 500 color and b/w photos • 224 pp.
ISBN: 0-7643-0387-2 • hard cover • $45.00

Last Hope: The Blood Chit Story. R.E. Baldwin & Thomas Wm. McGarry. The story of the tools aerial warriors used to evade capture when forced down in enemy controlled territory, as told by the Blood Chit. This definitive history of Blood Chits from their infancy at the dawn of the air age through their maturity at the close of World War II was compiled from accounts provided by more than fifty veteran airmen and intelligence officers from around the world, and from more than seventy formerly classified government documents. Last Hope is for the casual reader and serious researcher alike, and is a valuable resource for the military and aviation enthusiast, collector, researcher, and museum curator.
Size: 8 1/2" x 11" • over 240 color and b/w photos • 224 pp.
ISBN: 0-7643-0222-1 • hard cover • $49.95

United States Navy Wings of Gold from 1917 to the Present. Ron Willis & Thomas Carmichael. Willis and Carmichael chronicle, in full color, the development of Navy wings, including variations in designation, design and makers from World War I to the present. Also included is a listing of 17,000 naval aviators by name and number up to 1942.
Size: 8 1/2" x 11" • over 400 color photographs • 224 pp.
ISBN: 0-88740-795-1 • hard cover • $49.95

United States Combat Aircrew Survival Equipment World War II to the Present: A Reference Guide for Collectors. Michael S. Breuninger. A detailed study of United States Air Force, Army, Army Air Force, Navy, and Marine Corps aircrew survival equipment. Items covered are: survival vests, leggings, and chaps, life preservers, survival (ejection) seat and back pad kits, personal survival kits and first aid kits, etc. Tag and label information is provided for each item.
Size: 8 1/2" x 11" • over 170 b/w photos, drawings • 208 pp.
ISBN: 0-88740-791-9 • soft cover • $29.95

Submarine Badges and Insignia of the World: An Illustrated Reference for Collectors. Pete Prichard. A complete compendium of the submarine badges of the world, dating from the Imperial Russian Naval Officer's Submarine School Graduation Badge of 1909 to the new South Korean Submariner's Badge issued in 1996. Covers all countries currently operating submarines as well as those no longer existing as political entities.
Size: 8 1/2" x 11" • over 400 color photographs • 136 pp.
ISBN: 0-7643-0255-8 • hard cover • $45.00

Seeds of Victory: Psychological Warfare and Propaganda. Richard D. Johnson. To the layman, this particular aspect of armed conflict has seldom been greeted with understanding, or even acknowledgment. As a reference source, this text is of historical significance, as it documents the many deceptive Psychological Warfare campaign methodologies and strategies used in Iraq. Seeds of Victory has already demonstrated its value within the professional realm of the Psychological Warfare community, since its having been officially adapted by the United States Army's Psychological Warfare Group Command as an instructional and reference work for use within their company-level units.
Size: 8 1/2" x 11" • over 400 color photographs • 288 pp.
ISBN: 0-7643-0349-X • hard cover • $49.95

Uniforms and Equipment of U.S Army Infantry, LRRPs, and Rangers in Vietnam 1965-1971. Paul W. Miraldi. A comprehensive guide to the history, development, wear, and use of uniforms and equipment during America's involvement in the Vietnam War. Using re-constructed photos the author recreates the look and appearance of the American Soldier in Vietnam. This book fills an important gap in the collector's reference library and will be invaluable for collectors, historians, reenactors, modelers, curators, and artists.
Size: 9" x 12" • over 600 color and b/w photographs • 208 pp.
ISBN: 0-7643-0958-7 • hard cover • $59.95

Orders, Decorations and Badges of the Socialist Republic of Vietnam and the National Front for the Liberation of South Vietnam. Edward J. Emering. The Orders and Decorations of the "enemy" during the Vietnam War have remained shrouded in mystery for many years. References to them are scarce and interrogations of captives during the war often led to the proliferation of misinformation concerning them. Covered are those Orders and Decorations now considered official by the SRV, as well as many of the obsolete awards bestowed by the DRV and the NLF. It also discusses many of the commemorative, political and local awards. Includes value guide.
Size: 8 1/2" x 11" • 190 color and b/w photos • 96 pp.
ISBN: 0-7643-0143-8 • soft cover • $24.95

Weapons and Field Gear of the North Vietnamese Army and Viet Cong. Edward J. Emering. Field gear and inert weapons and ordnance have long been popular items with militaria collectors. The Vietnam War by its very nature offers an incredible range and variety of these items for the interested collector. This book will help both the serious collector as well as those individuals interested in acquiring only a token piece of history to avoid potentially costly mistakes. A value guide is included.
Size: 8 1/2" x 11" • over 400 color and b/w photos • 160 pp.
ISBN: 0-7643-0583-2 • hardcover • $39.95

Viet Cong: A Photographic Portrait. Edward J. Emering. The Viet Cong have long remained a mystery even to those who fought against them during America's longest and most divisive war. They have been given many acronyms and slang names, and they have been portrayed in many guises by the American press and popular Hollywood films. This work will strip away the myth and mystery which surrounds the Viet Cong and, through the medium of their own candid photography, present them in human terms. A cultural obsession, photographs were taken wherever and whenever possible. On many occasions, Allied forces were able to capture such photos. It is from such sources that these photographs are made available, most for the first time ever, to the general public.
Size: 8 1/2" x 11" • over 290 b/w and color photos • 200 pp.
ISBN: 0-7643-0758-4 • hard cover • $39.95

Tiger Patterns: A Guide to the Vietnam War's Tigerstripe Combat Fatigue Patterns and Uniforms. Richard Denis Johnson. Vietnam era tigerstripe combat fatigues have always been a much sought after commodity. *Tiger Patterns* analyzes to the most minute degree, the finite variances which defined the many original, Vietnam-era tigerstripe patterns and uniform cuts and establishes dependable iden-

tification techniques and practices, whether your particular interests are as a historian, veteran, modeler, or collector and enthusiast.
Size: 8 1/2" x 11" • over 280 color and b/w photographs, line drawings • 264 pp.
ISBN: 0-7643-0756-8 • hard cover • $69.95

Camouflage Uniforms of European and NATO Armies 1945 to the Present. J.F. Borsarello. This full-color book covers nearly all of the NATO, and other European armies' camouflaged uniforms, and not only shows and explains the many patterns, but also their efficacy of design. Described and illustrated are the variety of materials tested in over forty different armies, and includes the history of obsolete trial tests from 1945 to the present time. This book provides a superb reference for the historian, reenactor, designer, and modeler.
Size: 8 1/2" x 11" • over 290 color and b/w photos • 120 pp.
ISBN: 0-7643-1018-6 • soft cover • $29.95

The Viet Nam Zippo: Lighters 1933-1975. Jim Fiorella. Among the books concerned with the Vietnam war and its collectibles, this is unique in quality and content. It provides not only hundreds of photos of authentic and counterfeit Zippos and the factory's own artwork, but also a concise outline of the war, lists of U.S. and Vietnamese ship and boat names, Allied in-country units, and a comprehensive dictionary translating important Vietnamese military terms so that old Zippo lighters can be interpreted today. Related advertising pieces, postage stamps, newspaper clippings, Vietnamese patches, and more will fascinate all readers.
Size: 8 1/2" x 11" • over 900 color photos, price guide • 192 pp.
ISBN: 0-7643-0594-8 • hardcover • $39.95

U.S. Navy and Marine Corps Campaign & Commemorative Medals. Edward J. Emering. This work provides an in depth overview of not only the history and development of each campaign medal, but also the historical significance of the events surrounding the establishment of each medal. The book also covers several of the more important commemorative medals often struck on a limited basis to account for the lack of appropriate official federal awards. This work, which is well organized and easy to read, proves to be an interesting and informative reference work for the collector of these Navy and Marine Corps medals. A value guide is included.
Size: 8 1/2" x 11" • over 180 color and b/w photos • 88 pp.
ISBN: 0-7643-0386-4 • soft cover • $19.95

Camouflage Uniforms of the Soviet Union and Russia 1937-to the Present. Dennis Desmond. A comprehensive guide to the history, design and use of camouflage field uniforms of the Soviet Union and Russia. This excellent reference contains factual and interesting material covering the earliest days of uniform development to the most recent issues of the Ministry of Internal Affairs, former KGB and Spetsnaz forces. This book fills an important void in the collector reference library that has been vacant far too long. Designed with both the militaria collector and Russophile in mind, this book is an easy to use picture guide to the most sought after collectible in the Soviet and Russian militaria field, and is a must for any serious collector or intelligence analyst interested in the former Soviet Union or Russia.
Size: 8 1/2" x 11" • over 200 color photographs • 160 pp.
ISBN: 0-7643-0462-3 • hard cover • $45.00

Uniforms of the Soviet Union 1918-1945. David Webster & Chris Nelson. For the first time a photographic study of the Soviet uniforms from the Revolution, Civil War, Purges, and the Great Patriotic War. Hundreds of full color highly detailed photographs of actual uniforms are combined with period black and white photographs. Actual uniforms of Marshals of the Soviet Union, to private soldiers of all services are to be found in this extensive volume.
Size: 9" x 12" • over 500 color and b/w photographs • 288 pp.
ISBN: 0-7643-0527-1 • hardcover • $69.95

MiG Pilot Survival: Russian Aircrew Survival Equipment and Instruction. Alan R. Wise. *MiG Pilot Survival: Russian Aircrew Survival Equipment and Instruction* explores the components and details of Russian survival science with color photographs, in depth descriptions, and a full translation of the exact manual – with original illustrations intact – as used by Russian aircrews in time of crisis.
Size: 8 1/2" x 11" • over 180 color photographs and line drawings • 96 pp.
ISBN: 0-7643-0130-6 • hard cover • $19.95

Lenin's Legacy: A Concise History and Guide to Soviet Collectibles. Martin J. Goodman. *Lenin's Legacy* combines a concise history of the Soviet Union with a study of its "symbolism," which until now has largely been hidden from the West. The book shows nearly 2000 items including pins and badges, orders and medals, busts and statues, table medallions and wall plaques, banners and flags, paintings and coins and many others. Subjects covered include political, communist party, Aeroflot, Soviet space programs, party congresses, Lenin, Soviet military forces and others. This book is designed not only for the collector, but also the historian. Prices are included to aid collectors.
Size: 8 1/2" x 11" • over 900 color photographs • 208 pp.
ISBN: 0-7643-1019-4 • hard cover • 59.95

Military Medals, Decorations, and Orders of the United States and Europe: A Photographic Study to the Beginning of WWII. Robert W.D. Ball & Paul Peters. Rare, seldom seen medals, decorations and orders, as well as those awards commonly encountered, with their intricate details captured in spectacular color. Descriptions and value guide give the reader the opportunity to indentify and grade their collections. Covered are medals from: Albania, Austria, Belgium, Bulgaria, Czechoslovakia, Denmark, Finland, France, Germany, Great Britain, Greece, Hungary, Italy, Luxembourg, Montenegro, Netherlands, Norway, Poland, Portugal, Romania, Imperial Russsia, Serbia-Yugoslavia, Spain, Sweden, Turkey, and the United States.
Size: 8 1/2" x 11" • over 500 b/w and color photos • 184 pp.
ISBN: 0-88740-579-7 • hard cover • $45.00

Historical Record of the 14th (King's) Hussars 1715-1900. Col. Henry Blackburne Hamilton. This reprint of the 14th (King's) Hussars unit history was first published in 1901 and appears here in a new quality edition. The 14th (King's) Hussars, originally formed in 1715 as Dromer's Dragoons and later as the King's Light Dragoons, was one of the most distinguished regiments in the British cavalry with battle honors earned in the Peninsular War, Punjab, Persia, Central India, and South Africa. This complete history is presented chronologically and details the commanders, operations and uniforms from 1715-1900, and is complemented with superb full color plates of uniforms and standards, and duotone photographs of the regimental commanders during this period. Detailed maps show operational campaign details.
Size: 7" x 10" • 33 duotone photographs, 16 color uniform plates, 12 maps • 736 pp.
ISBN: 0-7643-0351-1 • hard cover • $59.95

Uniforms of the Republic of Texas And the Men that Wore Them 1836-1846. Bruce Marshall. Only Texas, of all the states, can boast of a heritage that includes the army and navy of an independent nation. Its regulars were backed up by a militia described as "the most formidable, for their numbers, in the world." Contrary to the image projected by Hollywood and most historians, even in Texas, they were smartly uniformed and equipped with the latest in weaponry. With his internationally-honored art, Bruce Marshall has recreated the uniforms in twenty-six full color illustrations, supplemented by fourteen photographs – including the only two known of uniformed officers of the Texas army and navy.
Size: 8 1/2" x 11" • 26 color plates, over 30 b/w images • 88 pp.
ISBN: 0-7643-0682-0 • soft cover • $19.95

Nighthawks: Insider's Guide to the Heraldry and Insignia of the Lockheed F-117A Stealth Fighter. Patrick Allen Blazek. This book details the heraldry of the Stealth Fighter beginning 10 years prior to its history-making flights over Baghdad during Operations Desert Shield and Desert Storm. It includes actual photos of many rare F-117A patches produced only for those intimately involved in the F-117A Program. Information dealing with the development of these patches and explaining their symbology are provided. It's also about the people and comaraderie involved. As a bonus, this book contains history and lineage of patches produced during the Lockheed Product Excellence Program's existence for the Engineering and Manufacturing organizations concealed deep within the walls of the Skunk Works.
Size: 8 1/2" x 11" • over 160 color photographs • 80 pp.
ISBN: 0-7643-0681-2 • soft cover • $24.95